Cover illustration by Markus Prime
Preface edited by Eric G. Hardy
Layout design by Bryon Summers

Library of Congress Control Number:  2016903537

ISBN-978-0-9972775-0-0 (DIGITAL)
ISBN-978-0-9972775-1-7 (PRINT)

Published by
MLNN Prime, LLC
**Br PLAYGROUND**
West of Ivy, LLC

# B.R.U.H.

# MARKUS PRIME

N7433.4.P748 A4 2016x
Prime, Markus, artist.
B.R.U.H.
[Brooklyn, New York] : MLNN
Prime, LLC, [2016]

# PREFACE:

I'm often asked for my personal and artistic philosophies, and I've found they can all be summed up in one word:

## B.R.U.H.

The following pages lend insight and inspiration into this philosophy, as these illustrations break down exactly what B.R.U.H. means:

## Black Renditions of Universal Heroes

You'll probably notice that all of them are women. I could've said heroine and you may ask why I don't use this word, but then I'd have some questions for you.

Why do we need to decipher a female hero from a male? Would you be upset if you were expecting Superman and Superwoman showed up? Would you take Wolverine less seriously as a woman? If Juggernaut was a giant woman pummeling dudes left and right, would that still appeal to you? Would you find some way to downplay it? What if the Pink Ranger was a guy and the Red Ranger was a woman? What if Sleeping Beauty was a man, waiting for a woman to come rescue him with a kiss?

Now let's add to that.

What if these heroes were not only women, but Black women? What if Naruto had Bantu knots and full lips with chestnut brown skin? What if the Hulk was tall and powerful with strong Yuroba features and a four-foot afro? Would it be so far-fetched to have more Pokémon trainers of color? Is it so ridiculous that I would like to see one or two Black Gundam pilots?

Why wouldn't there be more Black people in the Marvel universe if it were the universe that reflects the real world? It took forty-nine years to see Miles Morales, the first Afro-Latino Spiderman. Why is this even a big deal? Why do I have to ask these questions in 2016?

Cartoons were my first love. I was born in the late 80s, and one of my earliest memories was of the Teenage Mutant Ninja Turtles. I was obsessed. You name it, I had it: every episode on VHS, T-shirts, pajamas, bed set, curtains, toothbrushes, bath towels and every action figure I could find. My obsession was that of the typical American child in the throes of the iconic Murakami-Wolf studio's reign over children's animation. This may not seem like a big deal to most, but as I got older I came to a realization about this story that would forever change my perspective.

## What if Naruto had Bantu knots and full lips with chestnut brown skin?

As the story goes, the turtles befriended a young reporter in New York by the name of April O'Neil. In the story, most of us are accustomed to the fact that she is a middle-aged White woman just trying to make it. One day, much later as I learned the history of Kevin Eastman and Peter Laird's characters, I found that in the original comics April O'Neil was a woman of color. This changed so much for me and I didn't even realize it was a big deal... until it was.

Why did that have to change? I wonder who approached whom and said, "This story would be better if everyone was White," or even worse, "We're not going to make the story unless April O'Neil is White." This is arguably one of the biggest media franchises in history. Could that success been achieved if April was Black? The subject matter would've changed dramatically even in such a simple cartoon, adding depth and new directions for a story that could parallel the true evolution of America.

But that's just my opinion.

## A Black woman can be the most powerful character in her story without it being portrayed as out of the ordinary.

All I want is for this book to make you think. This is a small collection of parody illustrations, each from characters I grew up watching or enjoy today. Homage to the way illustration has pushed me to use my imagination more as an artist. Are you offended by the prospect of seeing your heroes depicted exclusively as Black women? If so, then this book is for you.

Women are the most underappreciated aspect of life in this world, and in my opinion Black women are even more overlooked. I can hardly remember any powerful Black women in the world of anime, American animation or even the comic book universe.

You may be thinking: Well the same goes for the Black man! This is true to an extent, but consider the fact that if a Black man struggles to be heard, a Black woman has to yell even louder than he does. By highlighting the power and beauty of the Black woman, I simply chose to be a part of the solution rather than to continue analysis of the problem. If I can somehow help put permanent, powerful, consistent images of Black women in these roles, perhaps more people will be comfortable with the idea of Black women being just as, if not more powerful than men.

The truth is that a Black woman can lead a story without needing a love interest. A Black woman can be the most powerful character in her story without it being portrayed as out of the ordinary. An entire group of Black women can be powerful, complex characters without being led by a male character or being overtly sexual for the purpose of marketing. This is simply my reasoning, my perspective, my vision.

Take each image in and create your own story as you delve further into this collection. Try to understand why I gave each character the features I did, why it makes sense in their world. I hope I inspire you like you inspire me. Enjoy.

- Markus Prime

**markusprime_** @markuspr1m3_
Africa is the greatest ghostwriter of all time.

**markusprime_** @markuspr1m3_
You matter.

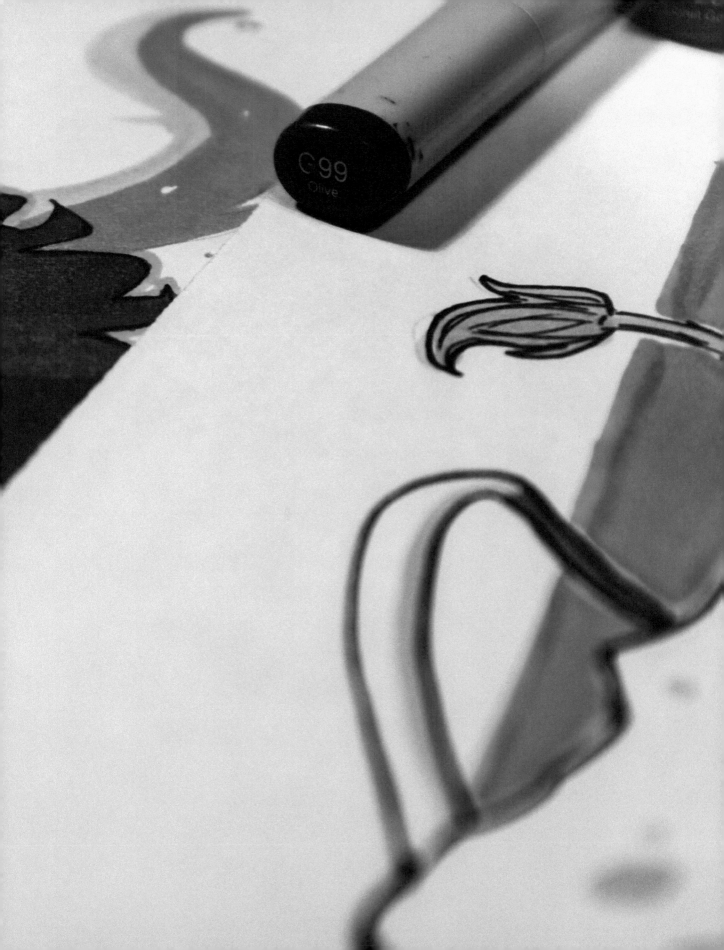

**markusprime_** @markuspr1m3_
Representation matters.

**markusprime_** @markuspr1m3_
Create what makes you happy.

**markusprime_** @markuspr1m3_
If they don't see you, make sure
they hear you.

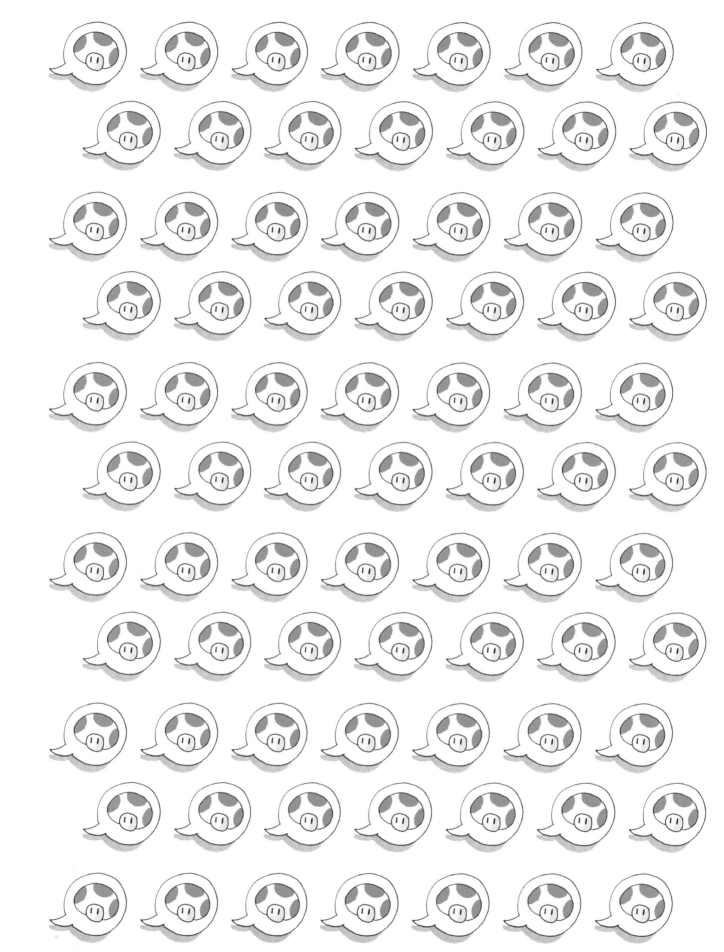

BRUH

**markusprimelives** And the winner of the #PeoplesChoice by a landslide is the ICE KING! You know it's gonna be a woman in my book now right? Look out for my upcoming book B.R.U.H. Thanks for participating! #BRUHPrime

**wordsofdivine** Yaaaas!

**thewearyboson** Can't EVEN wait!! #BRUHPrime

**ylmenkylmenk** I absolutely Love himmmmmmm  #adventuretime

**brooklyntillidie_** I don't think the ice king would mind being a girl

**markusprime_** @markuspr1m3_
Live with purpose.

**markusprime_** @markuspr1m3_
Trust your gift. Jump.

**markusprime_** @markuspr1m3_
Imagination is everything.

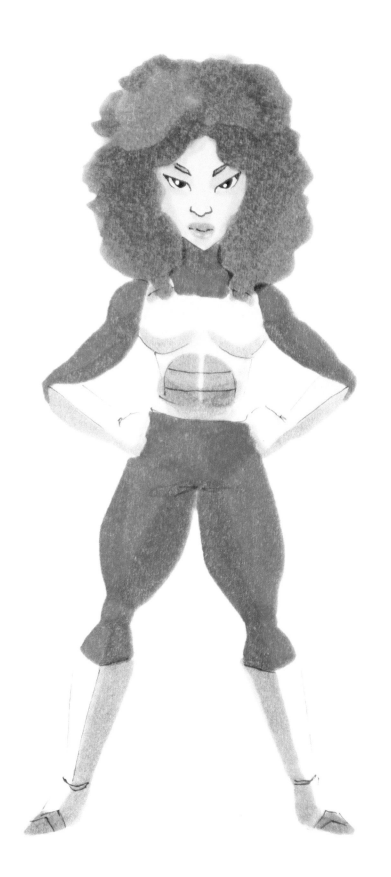

**markusprime_** @markuspr1m3_
There is no right or wrong way to ART.

**markusprime_** @markuspr1m3_
Art is my religion.

@MARKUS
PRIME
LIVES

@MARKUS PRIME LIVES
@MARKUS PRIME LIVES
@MARKUS PRIME LIVES
@MARKUS PRIME LIVES
@MARKUS PRIME LIVES
@MARKUS PRIME LIVES
@MARKUS PRIME LIVES
@MARKUS PRIME LIVES

@MARKUS PRIME LIVES
@MARKUS PRIME LIVES
@MARKUS PRIME LIVES
@MARKUS PRIME LIVES
@MARKUS PRIME LIVES
@MARKUS PRIME LIVES
@MARKUS PRIME LIVES

@MARKUS PRIME LIVES
@MARKUS PRIME LIVES
@MARKUS PRIME LIVES
@MARKUS PRIME LIVES
@MARKUS PRIME LIVES
@MARKUS PRIME LIVES
@MARKUS PRIME LIVES
@MARKUS PRIME LIVES

@MARKUS PRIME LIVES
@MARKUS PRIME LIVES
@MARKUS PRIME LIVES
@MARKUS PRIME LIVES
@MARKUS PRIME LIVES
@MARKUS PRIME LIVES
@MARKUS PRIME LIVES

@MARKUS PRIME LIVES
@MARKUS PRIME LIVES
@MARKUS PRIME LIVES
@MARKUS PRIME LIVES
@MARKUS PRIME LIVES
@MARKUS PRIME LIVES